An Anthology of Piano Music Volume IV

The Twentieth Century

**Selected and Edited
by Denes Agay**

**With an Introduction
by Louis L. Crowder**

Head of the Department of Music
The University of Connecticut

Yorktown Music Press, Inc.
New York · London · Sydney

US ISBN 0.8256.8044.1
UK ISBN 0.7119.0315.8
US Complete Set 0.8256.8040.9
Library of Congress Catalog Card Number: 72-150252

Exclusive Distributors:
Music Sales Corporation
24 East 22nd Street, New York, NY 10010 USA
Music Sales Limited
78 Newman Street, London W1P 3LA England
Music Sales Pty. Limited
27 Clarendon Street, Artarmon, Sydney NSW 2064 Australia

Printed in the United States of America by
Vicks Lithograph and Printing Corporation
10/84

FOREWORD

The content of AN ANTHOLOGY OF PIANO MUSIC was selected from the keyboard literature of nearly four centuries. From the early Baroque to the present, through the works of 139 composers, all important musical idioms and modes of expression are represented. The material is divided into four volumes:

Volume I —THE BAROQUE PERIOD — from the end of the 16th century
(late Renaissance) to the end of the 18th (Rococo).

Volume II —THE CLASSICAL PERIOD — the second half of the 18th
and the early 19th centuries. (Haydn, Mozart, Beethoven
and their contemporaries.)

Volume III —THE ROMANTIC PERIOD — piano music of the 19th century.

Volume IV —THE TWENTIETH CENTURY— piano works by major composers
of our time.

It is hardly necessary to point out that no rigid stylistic boundaries separate these volumes and that, inevitably, there is some chronological and idiomatic overlapping. The works of the sons of Johann Sebastian Bach, for instance, which conclude the baroque volume could have been placed as well at the beginning of the classical section. Fauré, Sibelius, Rachmaninoff and others, who wrote during the late 19th and early 20th centuries, could have been included in either the romantic or the contemporary volume, depending on whether we consider their modes of writing or their life-spans as a yardstick. It is better, then, to view this Anthology, and for that matter, the entire music literature, not as a succession of clearly separated and defined plateaus, but rather as a broad, ever-flowing stream with many branches and tributaries. This stream, the literature of keyboard music, is so vast that even the impressively sizable body of this Anthology, amounting to nearly one thousand pages, can represent but a small fraction of it.

This fact alone can give a hint of the difficult process involved in selecting the contents of these volumes and of the often thorny decisions the editor had to make. Which Preludes and Fugues of Bach's "48" should be chosen? Which Sonatas of Mozart and Beethoven should be included? Are the contributions to keyboard romanticism of an Heller or an Alkan substantial enough to warrant inclusion? Is the amount of space allocated to a certain composer in proper ratio to his importance? These and other similar questions had to be answered, always keeping in mind the main purpose of this Anthology and constantly trying to achieve a reasonable balance between the aesthetic, pedagogic, and historic considerations on the one hand and the dictates of space limitations on the other.

The purpose of this Anthology is twofold: to present a comprehensive survey of the entire keyboard literature through works which are appealing and representative, without being too demanding from either a musical or technical point of view; and to furnish an academically sound and varied teaching and performing library. The grade level of the contents ranges from easy to advanced, with the bulk of the material falling well within the intermediate grades. We felt that this segment of the piano repertory can furnish the most suitable materials for our multi-purpose collections. For this reason, works demanding utmost musical maturity and technical virtuosity, such as the late Sonatas of Beethoven, the lengthier concert pieces of Schumann, Chopin, Liszt, and others were not included.

All selections are based on authentic sources and are in their original forms. Tempo, dynamic, and expression marks in small print or in parentheses are editorial additions and should be regarded as suggestions rather than rigid directions. In line with our aim to give the player an authentic as well as a practical edition, the less familiar ornamental signs, especially those of the English virginalists and the French clavecinists, were replaced by the equivalent and better known symbols of the German Baroque (J. S. Bach). There is a review of these ornamental signs and their execution on page 18 of our baroque volume. To aid the performer in avoiding the often puzzling problems involved in the recognition and correct interpretation of *long appoggiaturas,* these signs have been written out in conventional notation throughout the baroque and classical volumes.

The main body of this Anthology is compiled from the music of the great masters. Included are not only their well-known repertory pieces, but also other of their representative works which are seldom found in similar collections. We have also included a number of relatively unknown, nonetheless delightful pieces by a few minor masters. These composers were perhaps not creative minds of the first magnitude but they did produce occasional works of striking beauty, especially in the smaller forms, and should be entitled to the measure of recognition offered by an anthology.

We hope to have succeeded in conveying the many factors, viewpoints and considerations which guided the selection of materials for these volumes. The final choices inevitably reflect, of course, the personal taste and didactic principles of the editor. It should be noted, however, that the process of compilation also included extensive consultations and discussions with many distinguished pianists and educators. To them, too numerous for individual mention, we express our heartfelt thanks and gratitude. In addition, we are deeply indebted to Mr. Eugene Weintraub, for his invaluable editorial help, to Mr. Herbert H. Wise, for his patience and wisdom in guiding this large publication project, and to Professor Louis L. Crowder, for his richly illuminating commentaries on the styles and performance practices of each period.

October 1970   DENES AGAY

CONTENTS

Music

Antheil, George

Bartók, Béla

Casella, Alfredo

Cowell, Henry

Creston, Paul

Debussy, Claude

Einem, Gottfried von

Granados, Enrique

Gretchaninoff, Alexander

PIANO MUSIC OF THE TWENTIETH CENTURY by Louis L. Crowder

Depending on one's sympathy or lack of it for what he hears in contemporary music, our century might be described either as a richly imaginative period offering endless variety, or as one of utter chaos. There is no doubt that our new music is kaleidoscopic. We have lost the relative unanimity of purpose, outlook, and ideals that was characteristic of the romantic era. And in point of diversity at least, we are repeating the confusion of the Baroque. Many things have been started in our time; some have been abandoned, and others thrive. Even some inherited nineteenth-century attitudes still cling tenaciously to an existence that the times have outgrown. Characterizing our era is thus more baffling than it was with the baroque, since we see our confusion from within and can only guess its outcome.

During the first forty years of the twentieth century, late romantic composers throve side by side with startling innovators. We played the music of Rachmaninoff and found nothing to disturb the romantic vocabulary we had inherited from Chopin and Liszt. Even pianistically we used virtually the same techniques. However, within these very decades, Debussy had finished his demolition of the old rules of harmony and form, and had invented his own language, as French as it was Romantic. The Viennese group, Schönberg, Webern, and Berg, had carried Wagner's chromaticism and dissolution of tonality to its inevitable conclusion and the twelve-tone system was born. Bartók had achieved the ultimate in dissonance and used it to startling dramatic effect in his evocations of Eastern-European folk music. Hindemith had evolved still another set of grammatical principles ideal to his neo-classical preferences, and was basing on them a new polyphonic style as sturdy as Bach's. And all the while a new generation of Russians produced music more and more infused with dissonance and harmonic unorthodoxy, but still basically romantic.

Amid all this wild divergence of esthetic standards and techniques, there appeared the ultimate in revolution—electronic music, sounds produced by electronic means and recorded permanently on tape. In this direct connection between composer and "performance" we were confronted for the first time by what seemed a threat to the very existence of the performer in the traditional sense. Then, as the computer joined this electronic orchestra, we wondered whether the composer himself might not be threatened with elimination.

Finally, as a sort of half-serious nose-thumbing postscript to the whole period has appeared *aleatory* (chance) music, in which the "composer" entrusts part of what used to be his task to chance and its operation through the performer, who becomes a sort of partner in the creative process. At its more serious levels, aleatory music does not deserve levity; usually some element or elements of the music are notated—rhythm, pitches, or tone durations—with others left to the performer. The absolute ultimate—selecting a title and then leaving the entire process to chance, in complete contradiction of the very nature of composition—has not seriously been tried. One should remember that the aleatory is not strictly new. An element of chance has entered into any musical performance, such as Jazz, involving simultaneous improvisation.

None of us knows of course which of these various routes the main stream of music will follow. Will all of us who perform be obsolete by the year 2050? Or will one or the other of the non-electronic trends become the channel of the future leaving the others to disappear?

Partial answers are already appearing to some questions. Fear of the "electronic peril" is proving ungrounded. The tape and the synthesizer are now recognized as new instruments and nothing more, instruments to be used as the composer would use the violin. In fact much of present day use of the electronic media is in combination with live performers on conventional instruments. In spite of many interesting compositions using electronic sounds exclusively, I suspect that works using the combined media may prove more lasting; they are certainly the more interesting now.

It must be emphasized that the computer is also merely a tool. No composer uses it as a sort of robot to produce a composition. An electronic work is simply "realized" or entrusted to tape with the help of the computer, thus saving the composer untold drudgery. Programming for the computer is still arduous, but nothing compared with the cut-and-splice methods of preparing tapes twenty years ago.

Of the other possibilities it is still too early to predict much except that, as always, everything changes. The original Viennese strict twelve-tone grammatical structure is becoming a matter of historical interest only; after all it's been around for over half a century. So called *serial* composers of today have generally relaxed Schönberg's rules or changed them to suit their own needs, much as Beethoven did the sonata form. Probably the twenty-first century will think of our time as having achieved a merging of the virtues of serial techniques with those of other possibly unforeseen developments.

Hindemith's innovative system, after having an immense impact on a generation of his pupils, still exerts a strong pedagogical influence through his theoretical writings, although as a strict compositional procedure it is largely abandoned. However, since some of the finest music of the twentieth century is Hindemith's, his influence is sure to be lasting.

Unlike Schönberg or Hindemith, Bartók developed no group of followers on the same scale, and cannot be said to have founded a "school." But again, his is some of the greatest music of the century, perhaps more important than the others. His complete liberation of the dissonance has probably destroyed forever any misgivings even the most conservative composer may have felt about its use. His influence will continue to be felt even in the works of some composers who may be unaware of its presence.

Minor trends have come and gone. Nationalism, evidenced in the Spanish works of Albeniz and Granados, in the music of Dvořak and the subsequent generation of Czech composers, or in the American music of Roy Harris and Charles Ives, has subsided, leaving us in debt for much beautiful music to a wide range of composers of varied stature. Sibelius, a sort of one-man representative of Beethoven and Brahms in the twentieth century, left us with works of massive dimension, complete integrity and a very personal brand of Nordic flavor.

Immediately after World War I Jazz began to exert an irresistable fascination for a number of European composers, long before it was considered worthy of serious attention by composers of the United States. Frenchmen, including Ravel, Milhaud and others, Germans such as Toch and Hindemith yielded to its then exotic appeal and wrote many works employing what they conceived as a jazz idiom. Later, beginning in the 1930's, numerous Americans (Harris, Barber, Copland and others) adopted elements of Jazz and continued to do so well into the fifties. The conscious use of Jazz seems to have diminished, at least for the present, although some of its flavor will always pervade American music, often not readily recognizable through being so thoroughly assimilated.

Two other short-lived "movements" made their appearance, *Pandiatonic Music* and *Polytonality,* both with roots in Debussy and elsewhere. Pandiatonicism limits itself to the tones of the diatonic scale, with no accidentals, and from it employs a wider range of combinations, both in chords and in melodic patterns, than was possible with traditional harmony. Polytonality exploited the bizarre effects obtained by the simultaneous use of supposedly incompatible tonalities. Both devices have ebbed in importance and have left hardly a trace except their continuing use in a non-systematic way by various composers as part of a larger vocabulary.

The present courtship of Indian and other Eastern musical systems is largely a hot-house cultivation, probably the outgrowth of a rapturous beating of the ethno-musicological drum in some of our universities. Its weakness lies in the assumption that the sophistication of centuries and the technical intricacies of an instrument that needs a lifetime of study can be absorbed by American students in a relatively short time. The interesting adoption of the *sitar,* along with much of Eastern mysticism and philosophy, by what was known a few years ago as the "hippie" culture has apparently been the cause of some dismay among the serious Indian performers who introduced this music in America.

Attitudes Toward Contemporary Music

One can solve the problem of attitude very simply by adopting a stern conservative position and refusing to see any value in any music closer to us than Rachmaninoff. Or, equally illogically, one can utter paeans of joy at every avant-garde manifestation, including perhaps the actual performance some years ago of a "composition" which included clipping neckties from and squirting toothpaste at the audience.

Difficult though it is, I think we all have to make choices, to form evaluations, and if necessary, to admit that we have at some points been mistaken. This is our only opportunity for the really basic, primary self-education that has been the problem of every generation since the classical era. Then, fortunately, everyone knew at least what music was like, and standards for its judgment were recognized.

Unfortunately the logic and order of Classicism did not survive the end of the era. With Romanticism came shocks to the musical consciousness of Europe on a scale not seen before. Late Beethoven was sometimes considered insane. Schumann was derided in many quarters. Berlioz was for a time beyond the pale of musical gentility. Naturally the public took sides, for or against each. Later Wagner went through the same ordeal, then Debussy. The validity of each forward step by every original composer was fought for or against by all the individuals who heard their music. And many a forward step was denounced by the conservatives as a step backward.

In the cases of composers who survived, we may assume that their backers were right and their detractors mistaken. And the supporters of many a widely acclaimed composer whose reputation has since collapsed were no doubt wrong. But what of the concert goer of 1890 who cheered Wagner on Wednesdays and, with equal fervor, Anton Rubinstein on Fridays? Should we recoil from the possibility of appearing ridiculous two generations hence because we failed to recognize genius when we heard it, or equally deplorable, because we cheered for a rising star that flickered out? Hardly! Even Schumann made mistakes of judgment occasionally. Certainly indiscriminate praise of everything new can do as much harm as good.

The important thing is not our personal box-scores of "right" and "wrong" judgments on contemporary music. In the first place one would have to wait fifty years to know the results. The really important things are, first, that we listen to everything new, and secondly, that we not be afraid to form our own—not someone else's second-hand—judgment of what we have heard. If we think it is great music, we should cheer in spite of the sneers or cat-calls around us. And if we think it reeks, we should say so. If we are not sure, we should hear the work again. This is necessary in any case; we might just possibly reverse our opinion in either direction. After all, Rellstab, one of the most noted critics in Europe, could see in Chopin only "strange tonalities, unnatural chord positions, preposterous combinations." But he made the mistake of never changing his opinion.

The collective judgment of individual listeners will in the long run determine what of contemporary music will survive, and this may not be in accord with "official" (meaning usually "critical") opinion. If Debussy had depended on the official opinion of his day, he would have been quickly forgotten. Not that immediate popular opinion is more reliable either, particularly when one thinks of the audience reaction to the first performance of many great works.

Actually it is the musicians who assure the survival of music in any era, and it is they who will determine what of today's new music will live. Our opinions, in other words, whether we wish it or not—not the opinions of the average listener nor the opinions of the critics—will be decisive. The only requisite is that our opinions be honest and fearlessly expressed.

Performing Contemporary Music

Absolutely no generalizations can be made concerning the performance of twentieth century music. Debussy needs a suave, gently controlled, but rigidly accurate technique, coupled with the most sophisticated pedalling ever required.

Hindemith demands a clarity of treatment which seems to combine the techniques of both Bach and Mozart. Bartók asks at times for a fearlessly percussive approach to his music, at others for some of the delicacy of Debussy. The recent Russians demand the usual Russian octave and chord techniques, brilliance in the fingers, and rigid rhythmic control.

More recent pianistic problems in the music of the post-twelve-tone serialists include a tendency toward excessive and sudden changes in dynamics, tempo, and rhythm, often presenting fantastic difficulties to the pianist on first encounter. However, after the unaccustomed has been mastered, what remains often presents less pianistic difficulty than Ravel or Mozart.

Actually, in its many-faceted variety, the music of the twentieth century presents every pianistic problem known between 1700 and 1940, with several new ones added since then. Whether this is a hopeless set of obstacles or a challenge depends on the pianist to whom it presents itself. Increasing numbers are finding the problem fascinating, exciting, and rewarding.

This Volume

Each of the divergent trends of twentieth-century music is well represented in this volume by compositions ranging widely from Prokofieff's *Moonlit Meadows*, which stylistically could have been written in 1870, to several examples of the twelve-tone technique.

The European vogue of Jazz is to be found in Milhaud's *Rag-Caprice* and Gottfried von Einem's *Allegro*. Its later American development is apparent with indigenous subtlety in an *Andante Cantabile* from a Piano Sonata by Howard Swanson.

Other national trends are strongly present in Villa-Lobos' *O Polichinelo* which has a delightful Brazilian flavor, and of course in Turina's *Clowns*, whose antics have echoes of Flamenco. Equally Spanish but in more suave, highly distilled idiom is Granados' *The Maiden and the Nightingale*, one of the best of all Spanish pieces by Spanish composers.

A large representation of Russian composers is inevitable since much of the best music of the century has been theirs. Prokofieff offers the well-known *March* from his "Music for Children" and several of his almost-impressionistic *Visions Fugitives*. Rebikoff, whose music usually offers an authentic turn-of-the-century Russianism, is represented by *Shepherd Playing his Pipe*, with its faint affinity to Debussy.

Kabalevsky, whose pieces for children are among the best ever written, is represented by several works of which I seem to prefer his *Prelude No. 15*. Other Preludes by Scriabin and Shostakovich clearly indicate the general trend of Russian music from the early years of the century with its turgid emotionalism to the recent tendency toward wit, sarcasm, almost classical clarity. Stravinsky wrote relatively little music for piano, but those who enjoy his music will find bits of authentic flavor in the *Allegro Marziale* and in other selections from his set of easy pieces, *The Five Fingers*.

Witold Lutoslawski, Poland's leading composer, who fits none of the categories of present day composition, is represented by two short pieces from *Bucolics*. I find them outstanding. Rieti, a widely respected Italian composer, presents two pieces of neo-classic clarity in essentially conservative style spiced with dissonance.

The Hungarian composers include some of more than nationalistic importance, even though the greatest of them, Bartók, used the folk music of his country as a point of departure in much of his composition. Even the *Sonatina* is solidly based on (Rumanian) folk elements. Kodály is even more persistently nationalistic, though another Hungarian, Ránki, preferred to seek more exotic national flavors elsewhere, and we find an authentic *Polynesian Lullaby* treated in a slightly Bartokian fashion. Bartók definitely transcends nationalism as no other composer of folk-based music was able to do.

Other twentieth century trends are present in several examples. The most charming bit of polytonality, to my mind, is Casella's *Carillon,* which here is a music box and not a bell tower. Toch uses a similar treatment for part of *The Prankster.*

Debussy is by this time so familiar that one wonders how his music could have stirred up such a furor; perspective *post facto* is always easy. As the first to challenge the exclusive validity of the Bach-based theoretical structure of the nineteenth century, he can be said to have opened the door to twentieth century music. During his lifetime his influence was enormous, even though the throng of young composers who became Debussists has with few exceptions disappeared. Several of Debussy's most loved pieces are included. There are, of course, many more pieces of equal beauty and usefulness awaiting discovery by venturesome students and teachers.

Ravel, though his name is often linked with Debussy's in statements about the "impressionists," offers more in contrast than in similarity. His music is usually "classic" as opposed to Debussy's romanticism, an excellent example being the *Sonatine*. The pianistic styles of the two composers vary widely also. Behind Debussy's most original treatments one sometimes detects a shadow of Chopin, whereas Ravel owes much to Liszt.

A very interesting synthesis of the Schönbergian twelve-tone system and the echoes of Impressionism is to be found in Hauer's *Resonances,* which exploit, by a continued and uninterrupted use of the damper pedal throughout a piece, some of the sonorous possibilities first explored by Debussy.

The twelve-tone school, which has become one of the dominant factors in twentieth century music, is still so much with us that we forget its roots go back almost as far as Debussy's. It was originally the product of one mind, Arnold Schönberg's. His frustration at what seemed to him the impossibility of further progress in music as it had evolved through Wagner, finally led him to abandon his own late-romantic inclinations and with them all the premises of music theory as it then existed. Tonality was abolished and with it all concepts of chordal relations, indeed of chords as such.

Music was thenceforth to be based only on the infinite possibilities for permutations to be found in a "tone-row," an arbitrary arrangement of the twelve tones included in one octave of the chromatic scale. Originally the rules were very strict—one tone must not be repeated before all were heard, etc. However, allowing for endless rhythmic variety and for all sorts of inversions and reversals, an astonishing range of possibilities presented themselves. The truly amazing fact is that not only did Schönberg invent a totally new musical language, but he wrote in it music of lasting importance. The two *Short Piano Pieces,* like the *Piano Piece* of Schönberg's pupil Webern, are easily grasped examples of twelve-tone or "serial" composition. Traces of twelve-tone influence are to be found in two pieces by Kadosa, and another example of fairly strict twelve-tone writing is the *Two-Voice Invention* by Jelinek.

Hindemith, confronted by the same problem as Schönberg, evolved a completely different solution. Tonality was retained, but with different rules governing its use in a highly polyphonic "neo-classic" setting. His *Dance Piece* is a charming example of his mature style.

American composers of several philosophies and periods are represented, aside from those already mentioned. Charles Ives, a notable "discovery" of the past thirty years, was an amateur composer, an almost cantankerously independent New Englander who refused during his lifetime to have his music published. He loved "American" sounds: brass bands, hymn tunes, and all sorts of special effects; and used them profusely in the most consciously "American" music ever written. *The Alcotts,* which forms the second movement of his Concord Sonata, evokes "the memory of that home under the elms. . . ." It begins in somewhat somnolent mood, punctuated by clock chimes, reaches some peaks of animation, and subsides to its original tranquility. (See also comments under "Alcotts" in Glossary.)

George Antheil shared with his earlier French counterpart, Satie, a reputation for being an "enfant terrible" of composition. Both talked more than they composed, deliberately poked fun at the establishment, and wrote music which today seems quite tame indeed. Antheil's short pieces are attractive and witty, and Satie's *Gnossienne* has genuine beauty. Paul Creston's compositional techniques have evolved continuously. The pleasing *Prelude* here included gives hints of MacDowell not to be found in his later works. William Schuman, one of our most notable present day composers is represented by two effective *Piano Moods* from a set of three.

Best of the American works included is, in my opinion, Piston's *Passacaglia.* Beautifully written for piano, it shows more than compositional skill and will, I think, become part of the enduring literature of the instrument.

Becoming familiar with even a part of the musical trends of our century is a formidable undertaking. This volume offers one of the best available introductions to the enjoyment of this endless variety of musical fare.

Prelude

Op. 11, No. 9

Andantino (♩ = 66)

Alexander Scriabin

18

Prelude

Op. 16, No. 4

Alexander Scriabin

Poem

Op. 31, No. 2

Alexander Scriabin

Allegro; con eleganza; con fiducia (♩= 84~88)

Shepherd Playing His Pipe

Op. 31, No. 8

Vladimir Rebikoff

Mouvement Plastique

Vladimir Rebikoff

Gymnopédie
No. 1

Erik Satie

Gnossienne

No. 1

Erik Satie

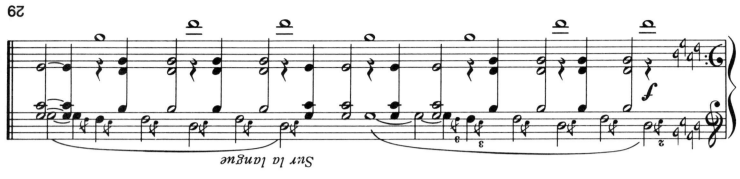

Sur la langue

Pas à Pas

Postulez en vous-même

Du bout de la pensée

Clair de Lune

from "Suite Bergamasque"

Claude Debussy

Andante très expressif

First Arabesque

Claude Debussy

40

Sarabande
from "Pour le Piano"

Claude Debussy

Avec une élégance grave et lente

Prelude

from "Pour le Piano"

Claude Debussy

Assez animé et très rythmé

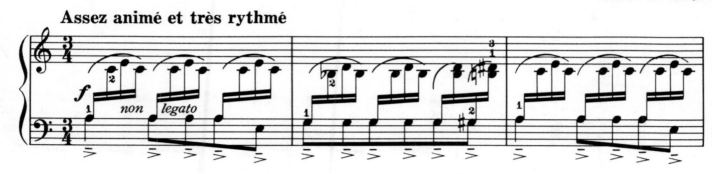

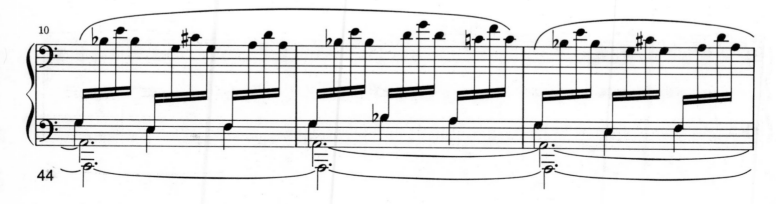

44

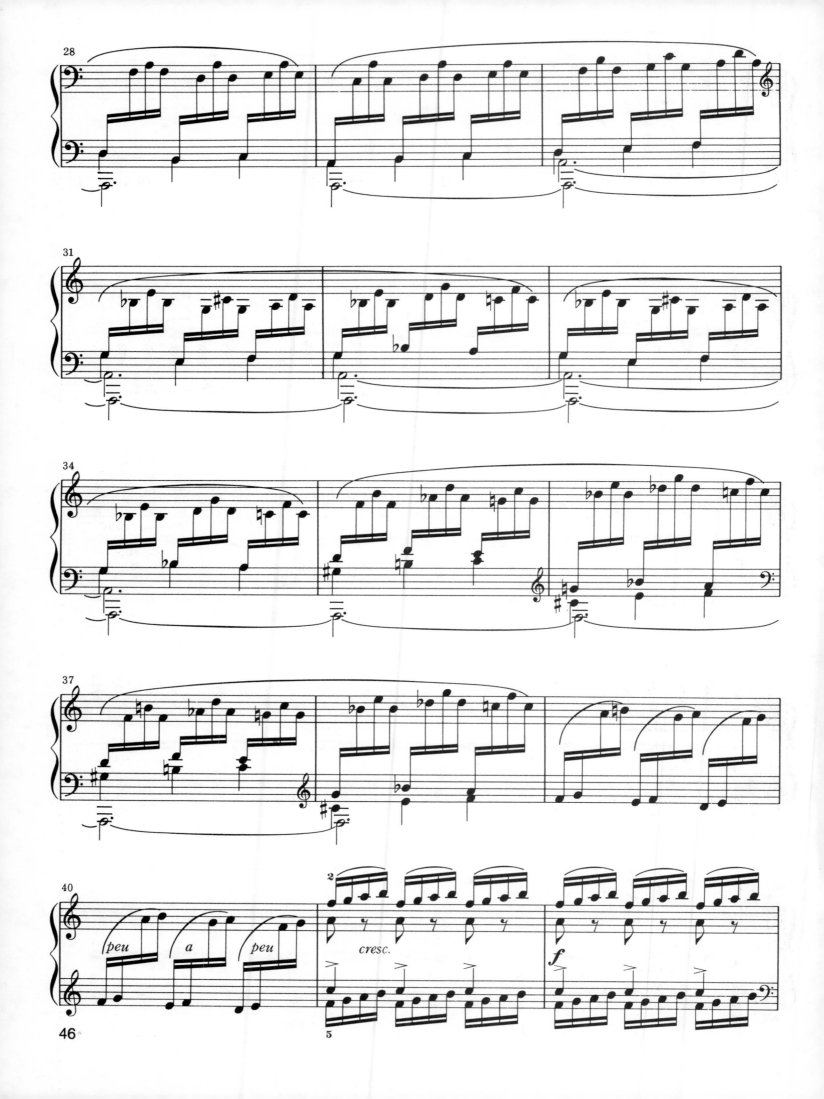

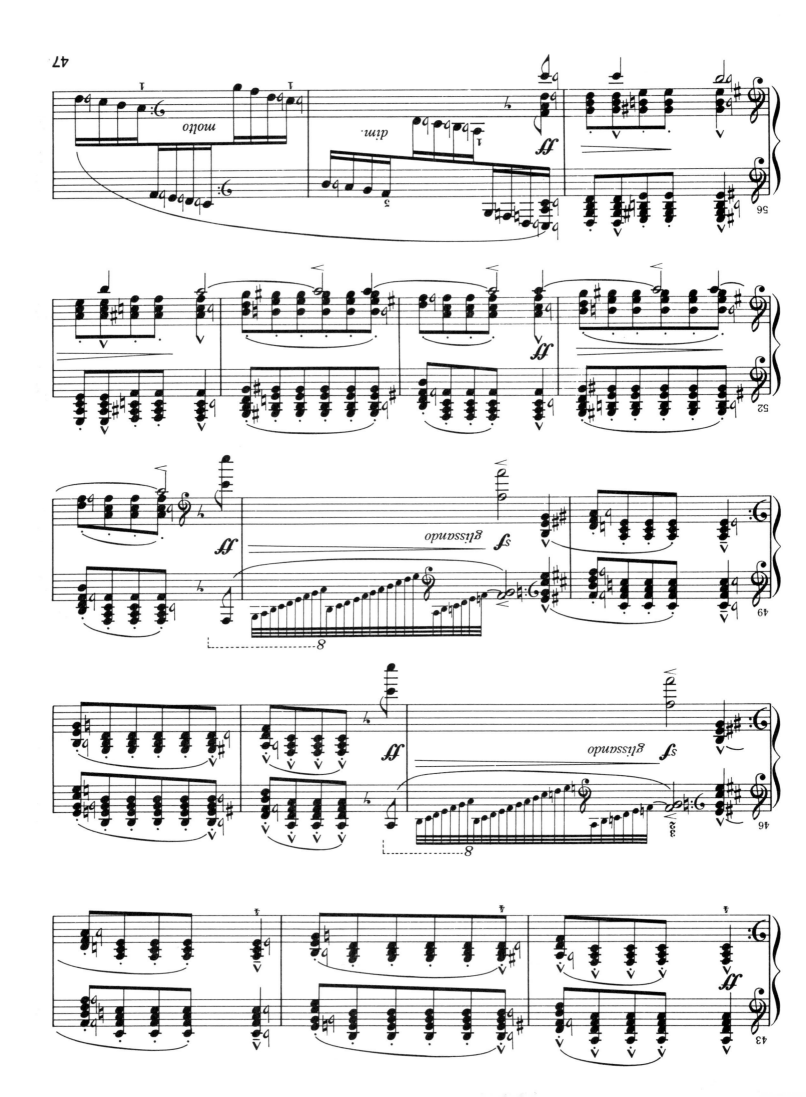

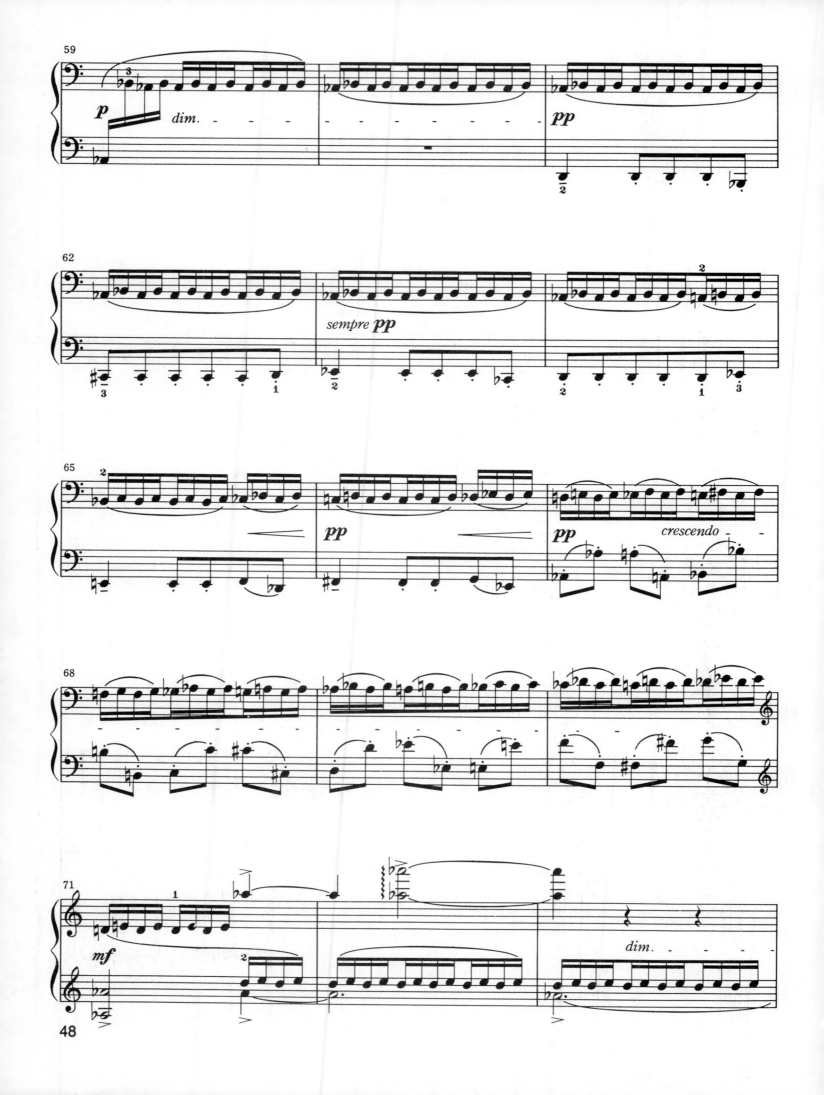

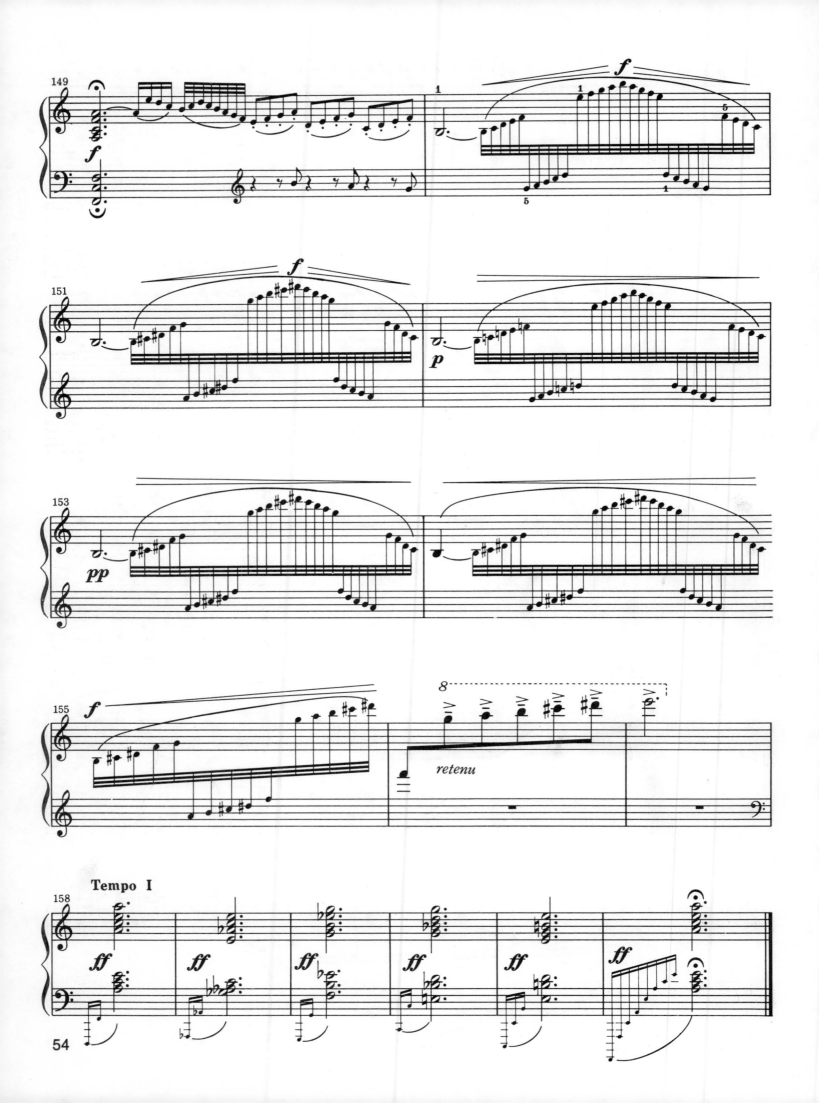

Valsette

Zoltán Kodály

Moderato Triste

No. 6 from "Nine Piano Pieces", Op. 3

Zoltán Kodály

Lotus Land

Op. 47, No. 1

Cyril Scott

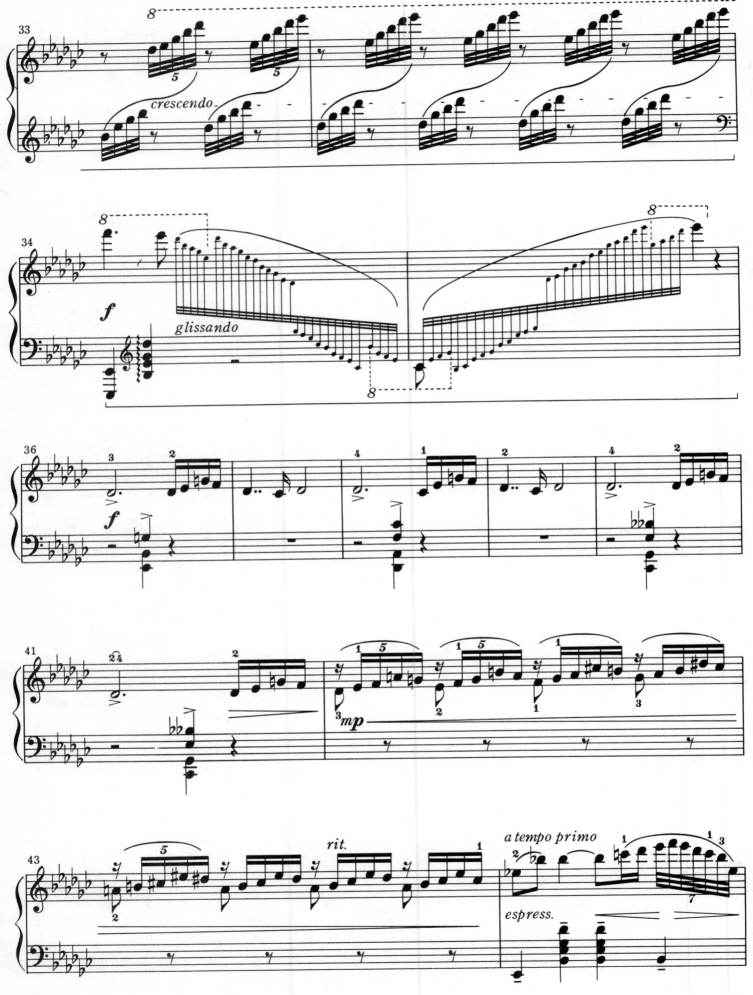

Sonatine

1

Maurice Ravel

2

Mouvement de Menuet

3

Lament

from "For Children", Book I

Béla Bartók

Andante

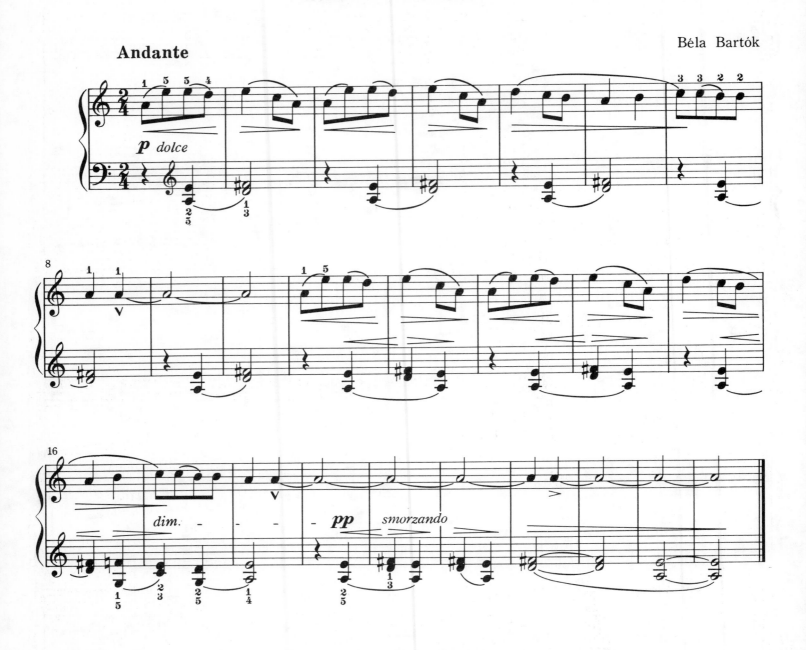

Play Tune

from "For Children", Book I

Béla Bartók

Allegro

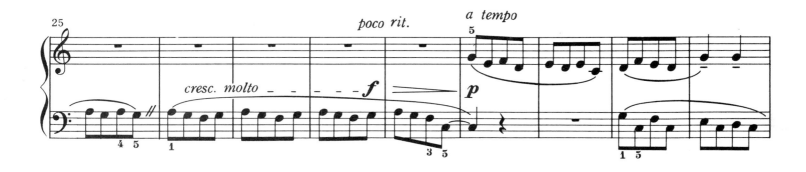

Dirge

from "For Children", Book II

Béla Bartók

Dance
from "For Children", Book II

Béla Bartók

Evening in the Country

from "Ten Easy Pieces"

Béla Bartók

Bear Dance

from "Ten Easy Pieces"

Béla Bartók

Sonatina
1
(Bagpipe)

Béla Bartók

2

(Dance)

3

(Finale)

Bagatelle No. 2

from Op. 6

Béla Bartók

Bagatelle No. 6

from Op. 6

Béla Bartók

100

"The Alcotts"

from Second ("Concord") Piano Sonata

Charles Edward Ives

In a gradually

excited way

l. h.

l. h.

accel.

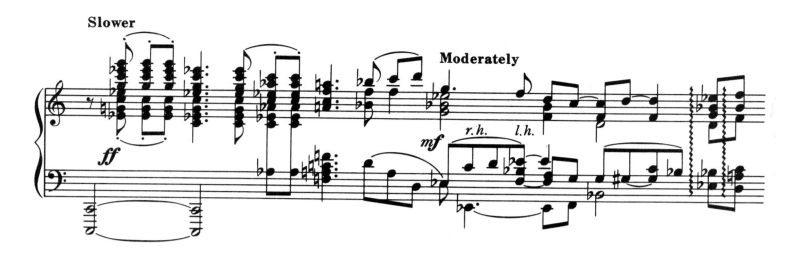

Two Short Piano Pieces

Op. 19, No. 2 and No. 4

Arnold Schönberg

1

2

Rasch, aber leicht (Fast, but light) (♩)

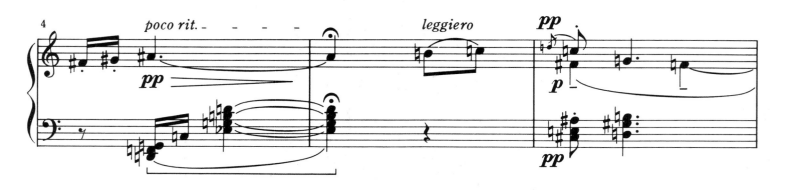

The Maiden and The Nightingale

from "Goyescas"

Enrique Granados

Andante melancólico

Etude
Op. 7, No. 3

Igor Stravinsky

Vivo

from "The Five Fingers"

Igor Stravinsky

(Alla Napolitana)

Lento

from "The Five Fingers"

Igor Stravinsky

(Arioso)

Allegro

from "The Five Fingers"

Igor Stravinsky

118

May Night

Selim Palmgren

Resonances

Nachklangstudien, Op.16, Nos.1, 4 and 5

1

Josef Matthias Hauer

* Accidentals refer always, even within the measure,
only to notes before which they are placed.

2

Pendelnd, wiegend, unrhythmisch, leise
(Softly swaying unrhythmic motion)

hold pedal throughout

3

Hüpfend, mäßig bewegt
(Hopping, moderate motion)

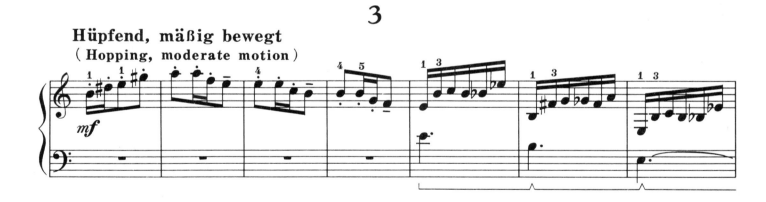

O Polichinelo

from Prole do Bêbê, No. 1

Heitor Villa-Lobos

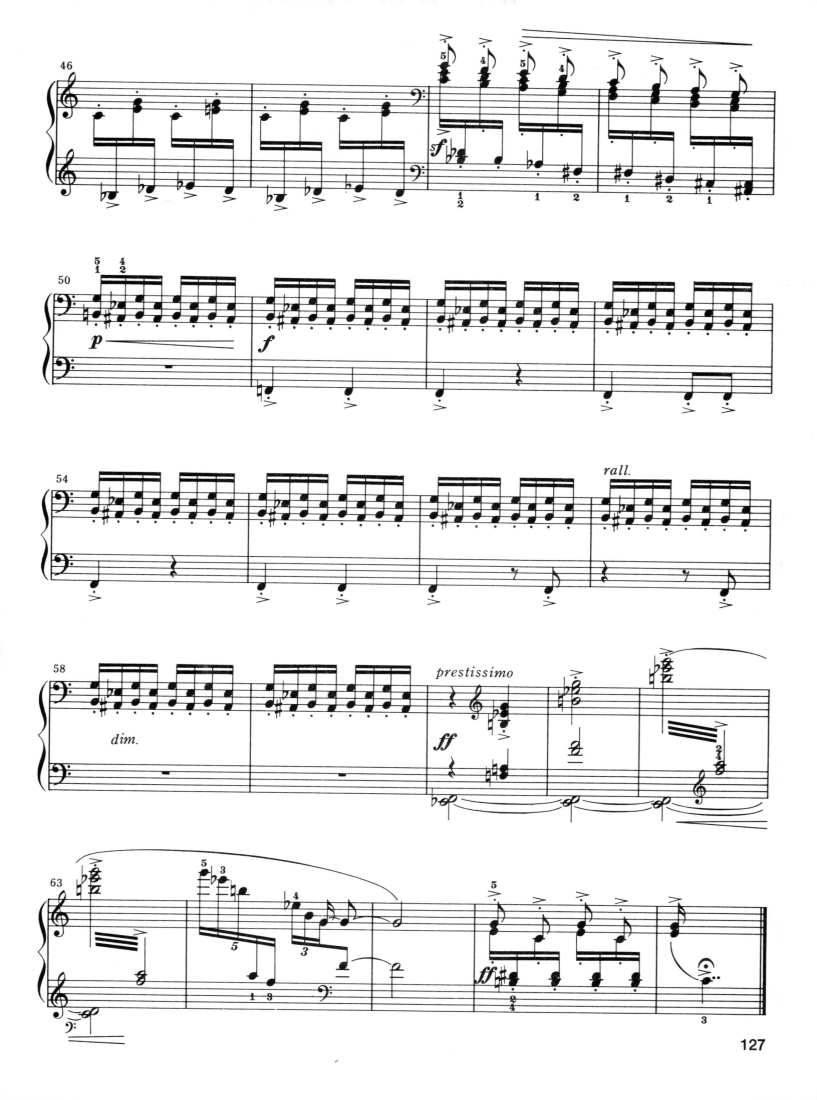

Little Prelude

Op. 109, No. 1

Alexander Gretchaninoff

On The Harmonica

Op.123, No.12

Alexander Gretchaninoff

Rag-Caprice

from " Trois Rag-Caprices "

Darius Milhaud

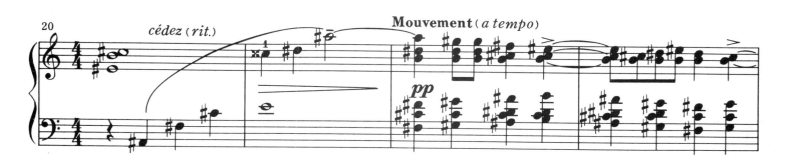

Siciliana
from "Eleven Children's Pieces"

Alfredo Casella

Carillon

from "Eleven Children's Pieces"

Alfredo Casella

Sempre più piano, ma rigorosamente in tempo.

Piano Piece

Op. 39, No. 5

Ernst Krenek

Dance Piece

from "Klaviermusik", Op. 37, II

Leicht bewegte ganze Takte (Lightly moving, ♩. = ca 66)

Paul Hindemith

Elegia

from "Six Short Pieces"

Vittorio Rieti

Sostenuto con dolore (♩ = 60)

Invenzione

from "Six Short Pieces"

Vittorio Rieti

Piano Piece

Klavierstück, Op. Posth.

Anton Webern

Im Tempo eines Menuetts

147

March
Op. 65, No. 10

Serge   Prokofieff

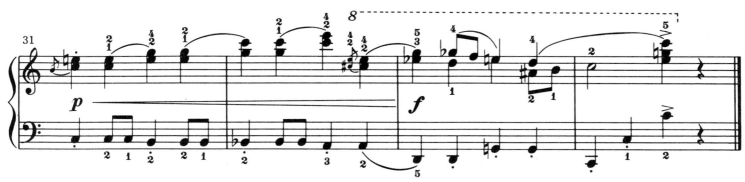

Moonlit Meadows

Op. 65, No. 12

Serge Prokofieff

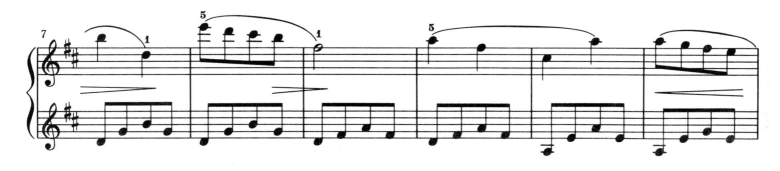

Légende

Op. 12, No. 6

Serge Prokofieff

152

153

Vision Fugitive No. 16

from Op. 22

Serge Prokofieff

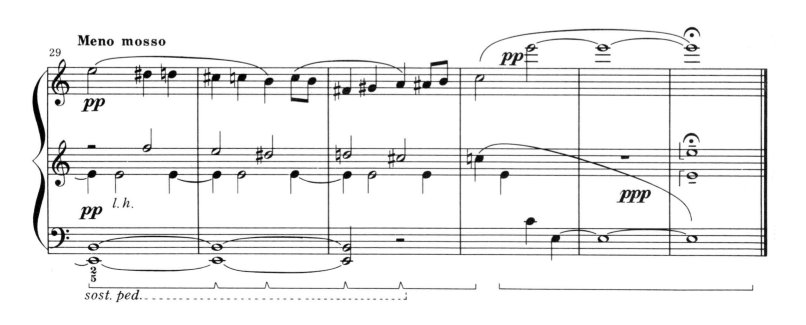

Vision Fugitive No. 10
from Op. 22

Serge Prokofieff

Ridicolosamente

157

Vision Fugitive No. 5

from Op. 22

Serge Prokofieff

The Prankster

"From a Small Town", Op. 49, No. 9

Ernst Toch

Bagatelle

Op. 5, No. 1

Alexander Tcherepnin

Clowns

from "The Circus"

Joaquin Turina

163

A Happy Fairy Tale

from "Six Children's Pieces"

Dmitri Shostakovich

Prelude
Op. 34, No. 16

Dmitri Shostakovich

Three Fantastic Dances

1

Dmitri Shostakovich

3

Seven Variations
on an Ukranian Folk Song
Op. 51, No. 4

Dmitri Kabalevsky

Allegretto scherzando

Theme

Var. 4

Var. 5 (**Poco sostenuto**)

p cantabile

176

Var. 6 (Vivo)

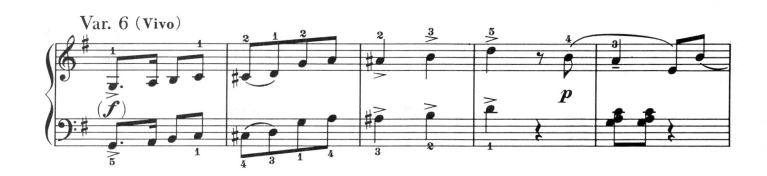

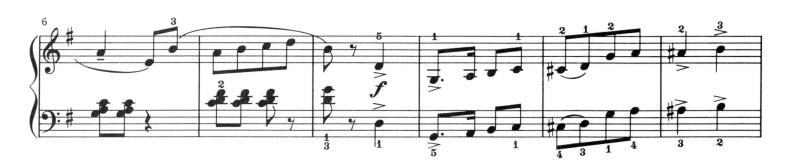

Var. 7 and Coda

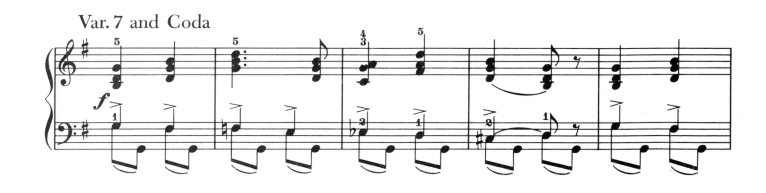

178

Rondo - Toccata

Op. 60, No. 4

Dmitri Kabalevsky

Prelude

Op. 38, No. 8

Dmitri Kabalevsky

Sonatina

C major · Op. 13, No. 1

I

Dmitri Kabalevsky

Allegro assai e lusingando

II

189

III

Prelude No. 2
from "Eight Preludes for Piano"

Frank Martin

Allegretto tranquillo (♩ = 80)
legg. ma sempre cantabile e non troppo dolce

un poco meno dolce

dolce legg.

cresc. poco a poco

196

Composer's note:
This piece should always be kept delicate and elegant until the forte section is reached,
without change in tempo. The intermittent low bass notes should be played without any particular stress.
Only at the end of the piece can they be a bit more accented, especially the organ point on the note B.

Piano Piece

from "Four Piano Pieces"

Gottfried von Einem

Passacaglia

Walter Piston

Prelude
Op. 38, No. 2

Paul Creston

Two-Voice Invention

On a Twelve-Tone Row

Hanns Jelinek

Moderato (Airily) ♩.= 60

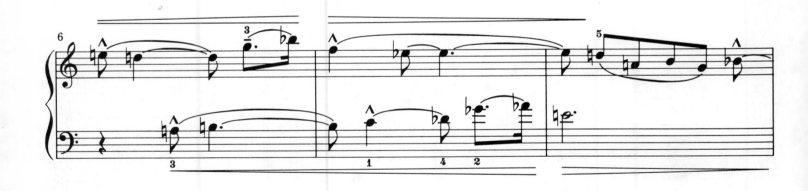

(ca 1:05)

Waltz
from "Adventures of Ivan"

Aram Khachaturian

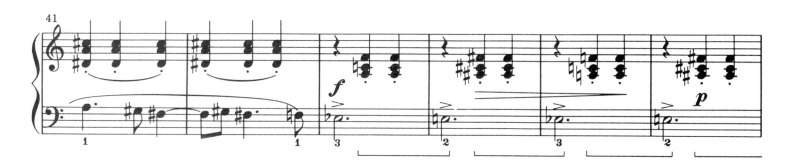

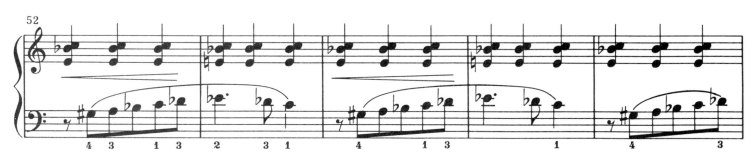

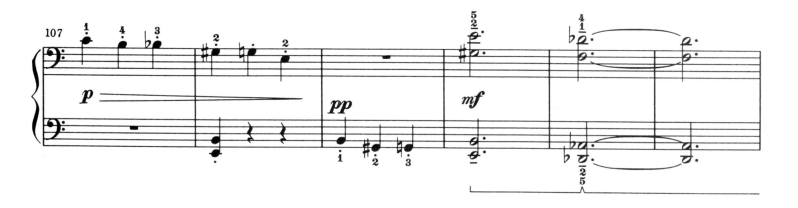

Andante Cantabile

from Piano Sonata

Howard Swanson

Shades of Blue

from "Sketches in Color"

Robert Starer

Bright Orange

from "Sketches in Color"

Robert Starer

Two Pieces from "Bucolics"

1

Witold Lutoslawski

Winter Lullaby

from "Piano Pastels"

George Antheil

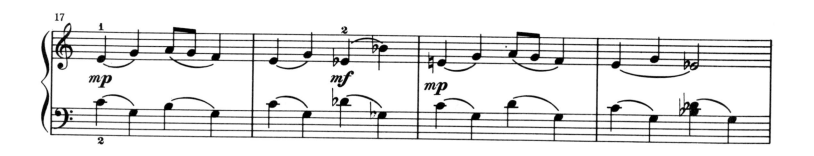

Dog - Cat Polka

from "Piano Pastels"

George Antheil

222

Piano Moods
1. Pensive

William Schuman

2. Dynamic

Poco meno mosso (♩ = ca. 144)

pressing forward

with utmost force

227

Sway Dance

Henry Cowell

Polynesian Lullaby

György Ránki

Laotian Flute

György Ránki

African Incantation

György Ránki

Two Pieces from "Kaleidoscope"

Op. 61, Nos. 4 and 3

Pál Kadosa

1

2

BIOGRAPHICAL SKETCHES OF COMPOSERS

Antheil, George, b. 1900, Trenton, N.J.—d. 1959, New York. "Enfant terrible" of American music in the twenties, settled down later to a calmer, deeper, and attractively melodic, almost romantic idiom. Some of his works display genuine humor, a rare quality in music.

Bartók, Béla, b. 1881, Nagyszentmiklós, Hungary —d. 1945, New York. Bartók represents the ultimate achievement in the interaction between a strongly nationalistic heritage and a richly imaginative musical mind. His early researches into old Hungarian, Rumanian, and Slovakian folk music colored his entire creative life—but on a level of originality and power never attained by any other composer. Of special disticition are his piano collections for children and students.

Casella, Alfredo, b. 1883, Turin, Italy—d. 1947, Rome. Leading figure of Italian music in our century; pianist, composer, editor, scholar. Neoclassical as composer, with polyphonic, antiromantic leanings. Had stimulating influence on younger Italian musicians.

Cowell, Henry, b. 1897, Menlo Park, Calif.—d. 1965, Shady, N.Y. A very prolific composer; pianist, teacher, writer on music. A dedicated champion of contemporary American works. A fearless experimenter and inventor of new sounds ("tone clusters"), new forms, new electronic instruments. His late works, somewhat deeper and calmer than the early ones, often have a modal character with undercurrents of pronounced folk influences.

Creston, Paul, b. 1906, New York. American composer of Italian origin. Traditionist, with touches of modalism. Essentially romantic, very skillful composer.

Debussy, Claude, b. 1862, St. Germain en Laye— d. 1918, Paris. One of the great innovators in music history, founder and foremost representative of French Impressionism. His liberating role made possible the new directions of much twentieth century music, and his was one of the strongest influences on the evolution of many of its styles. A deliberate breaker of musical conventions, he was influenced more by the symbolist poets and impressionist painters than by his musical contemporaries. His piano music, considered by some as the most important single *oeuvre,* since Chopin, enjoys a permanent, indispensable place in the literature.

Einem, Gottfried von, b. 1918, Bern, Switzerland. Austrian composer, living in Germany; known chiefly for his operas. The style of Einem's piano works is an interesting blend of various influences, Stravinsky, Prokofieff, and Jazz.

Granados, Enrique, b. 1967, Lerida, Spain—d. 1916, at sea (his ship torpedoed during World War I). Leader, with Albeniz, of the notable musical upsurge in Spain, in which a nationalist orientation based on folk music played a decisive part. His piano music is marked by rich post-romantic sonorities, great refinement, and deep poetic feeling.

Gretchaninoff, Alexander, b. 1864, Moscow—d. 1956, New York. Like Rebikoff, a transitional composer between 19th century romanticism and the Russian school of Stravinsky and Prokofieff. Wrote much excellent children's music of undiminished appeal.

Hauer, Joseph Matthias, b. 1883, Wiener-Neustadt, Austria—d. 1959, Vienna. Inventor of a twelve-tone system, possibly before Schönberg's. Although based on rigid theoretical principles, his music is not as dissonant as Schönberg's and shows some affinity with the works of Scriabin and Satie.

Hindemith, Paul, b. 1895, Hanau, Germany—d. 1963, Frankfurt, Germany. Left Germany in 1937, lived for many years in the U. S. and Switzerland. One of the finest composers of the twentieth century. Neo-classicist, contrapuntist in his treatment of form, Hindemith evolved his own highly original concepts of tonality and harmonic relationships. Continues to have strong influence on German and American composers of today.

Ives, Charles Edward, b. 1874, Danbury, Conn. —d. 1954, New York. A true non-conformist; pioneer in many directions. Used polytonality, polyrhythm, touches of atonality, and extreme dissonances in his treatment of very simple materials, often popular tunes or hymns. The resulting revolutionary sonorities have led to his being considered by many as the first truly original American composer. Some of his experiments antedate similar trends in Stravinsky and even Schönberg.

Jelinek, Hanns, b. 1901, Vienna—d. 1969, Vienna. Studied for brief periods with Schönberg and Alban Berg whose influences probably account for his strong preoccupation with the twelve-tone technique. The Invention in this volume is from his best-known work, a series of piano pieces evolved from ingenious manipulations of a single tone-row.

Kabalevsky, Dmitri, b. 1904, St. Petersburg, Russia. One of the best known and most respected protagonists of contemporary Russian music. A popular and versatile composer writing in an appealingly melodic, rather conservative idiom. His pieces for children are among the best ever written.

Kadosa, Pál, b. 1903, Léva, Hungary. Leading figure among Hungarian composers of the post-Bartók generation. His early style, deeply influenced by Hungarian folklore, gradually gave way to a more "objective," rather Hindemith-oriented, expressively forceful idiom.

Khatchaturian, Aram, b. 1903, Tiflis, Russia. Youthful drive, unabashedly melodic sentimentality, touches of Armenian and Oriental folk-influences are the ingredients of his idiom and also the reasons for his well-deserved wide popularity.

Kodály, Zoltán, b. 1882, Kecskemét, Hungary—d. 1967, Budapest. A devoted researcher of Hungarian peasant music, a close friend, often collaborator of Bartók. His idiom is firmly folk-based, often with impressionistic overtones. A great teacher, whose influence on pedagogy, particularly on the teaching of music to school children, is of immense importance.

Křenek, Ernst, b. 1900, Vienna. Has been a resident of the U. S. since 1938. Showed strong jazz influences in his early works; later adopted an atonal, twelve-tone idiom. Devoted follower of Schönberg.

Lutoslawski, Witold, b. 1913, Warsaw. Leading contemporary composer of Poland. Uses a very personalized twelve-tone idiom, with well-defined tonal centers.

Martin, Frank, b. 1890, Geneva, Switzerland—d. 1974 Naarden, Holland. Uses a modified twelve-tone system in a tonal orientation, quite opposed to the tenets of Schönberg. Some excellent piano music, though his reputation is largely based on vocal-orchestral works.

Milhaud, Darius, b. 1892 at Aix en Provence, France—d. 1974 Geneva. Prolific composer of the post- Debussy decades as one of "The Six" whose ideals led to a renunciation of Impressionism and a return to the classical ideals of Haydn and Mozart. Was strongly influenced by Jazz in the years following World War I, and by the music of Brazil through several years of residence in Rio. Resident of U. S. since 1940.

Palmgren, Selim, b. 1878, Björneborg, Finland—d. 1951, Helsinki. Significant Finnish composer, pianist, conductor. Studied abroad (with Busoni for a while), came to the U. S. in 1921 and taught composition at the Eastman School of Music; later returned to Finland. Piano works represent the major portion of his output. Most noteworthy are his smaller, lyric and melodically appealing pieces which show an inventive assimilation of Scandinavian folk elements.

Piston, Walter, b. 1894, Rockland, Maine. Outstanding composer and teacher who made a deep mark, in both capacities, on the development of contemporary American music. A neo-classicist, employing linear contrapuntal textures and venturesome harmonies within a tonal framework, he always is in superb control of compositional techniques. Wrote numerous important textbooks on aspects of theory.

Prokofieff, Serge, b. 1891, Sontsovska, Russia—d. 1953, Moscow. Ranks with Stravinsky as the greatest Russian composer of our time. Lived abroad from 1918 and settled again in Russia in 1934. A writer of exceptional creative powers, immense technical mastery, and high artistic integrity. In his autobiography Prokofieff lists five main characteristics of his style: "classical . . . innovative . . . propulsive . . . lyrical . . . jesting."

Ránki, György, b. 1907, Budapest. A pupil of Kodály, versatile, successful composer for many media. His is an attractive, often witty, and always easy-to-digest idiom, influenced by folk and jazz elements. His continued interest in ethno-musicology is manifest by the three charming miniatures in this volume, all based on authentic folk melodies of far-away lands.

Ravel, Maurice, b. 1875, Ciboure, France—d. 1937, Paris. In contrast to Debussy's individual romanticism, Ravel's music seems almost classical. Unlike Debussy's piano style, which explored new keyboard and pedalling possibilities, Ravel's is often based firmly on Liszt and on personal modifications of the great pianistic tradition. Still, it is strikingly original in sonority and pianistic effects. Considerable interest in folk music—Spanish, Hebrew, and American Jazz.

Rebikoff, Vladimir Ivanovich, b. 1866, Krasnoyarsk, Russia—d. 1920, Yalta. Late romantic in orientation, his music offers distinctive charm through its very personally flavored harmonies. Wrote some of the best children's music.

Rieti, Vittorio, b. 1898, Alexandria, Egypt. Widely respected Italian composer; a resident of the U. S. since 1940. Writes in a tonal, neo-classical idiom with polished craftsmanship and a certain elegant, melodious fluency.

Satie, Erik, b. 1866, Honfleur, France—d. 1925, Paris. Precursor of Impressionism in France. Later he turned away from this style. His avid antagonism to anything lush and pretentious in the arts, his sarcasm, plus a respect for simplicity led to a relatively small total of very individual piano works. Had great influence on an entire generation of younger composers, particularly "Les Six."

Schönberg, Arnold, b. 1882, Vienna—d. 1951, Los Angeles, Calif. Most revolutionary of twentieth century composers. His "atonal" innovations and the resulting twelve-tone system represented in the 1920's a complete reversal of all existing theoretical concepts. Had immense influence on many followers and on Western music in general.

Schuman, William, b. 1910, New York. Successful, widely respected composer, head of Juilliard School of Music from 1945 to 1962. Definite tonal centers are discernible in most of his works. Expressive, long melodic lines of lyric intensity or dramatic power — rhythmic exuberance, and touches of Jazz or other American folk influences are main elements of his idiom.

Scott, Cyril, b. 1879, Oxton, England—d. 1970, Eastbourne. Romanticist with impressionist tendencies; basicly concertive with a distinctive flair for individual harmonic treatments. His piano works often depict exotic topics.

Shostakovich, Dmitri, b. 1906, St. Petersburg, Russia—d. 1975 Moscow. Wrote one of his best works, the First Symphony, at the age of nineteen. His later career has been somewhat blighted by the repressive restrictions placed on all Russian art during the Stalin era. Remains one of the most versatile, facile, and natural musical talents of our time, who continues to contribute works of merit to all branches of music literature.

Scriabin, Alexander Nikolayevich, b. 1872, Moscow—d. 1915, Moscow. In his early works he was much influenced by Chopin. In later years daring harmonic experimentations led to a very personal type of pseudo-serial writing. Intense emotionalism preserves a basically romantic orientation, coupled with efforts to synthesize music, philosophy and religion.

Starer, Robert, b. 1924, Vienna, Austria. Settled in the U. S. in 1947. Prolific, versatile composer whose style is an effective synthesis of numerous contemporary trends. Winner of several prizes and awards.

Stravinsky, Igor, b. 1882, St. Petersburg, Russia—d. 1971, New York. Resident of the U. S. since 1939. Towering figure among contemporary composers. Style spans the great distance from his early, violent Russianism to neo-classicism, and finally to a characteristically personal, though basically Schönbergian, serial technique. Stravinsky, twice an emigré—for he left Russia after the revolution and was forced to leave his adopted country, France, during World War II—remains thoroughly a Russian. He has probably influenced twentieth century music as profoundly as any other composer. The piano is a relatively minor interest in the perspective of his vast output.

Swanson, Howard, b. 1907, Atlanta, Georgia—d. 1978, New York. Highly respected American composer; studied at the Cleveland Institute of Music and with Nadia Boulanger in Paris; received numerous fellowships, awards, and prizes. Prefers linear constructions and subtle tonal centers. His works have depth, intensity and an appealing lyrical quality.

Tcherepnin, Alexander, b. 1899, St. Petersburg, Russia—d. 1977, Paris. Another doubly emigrated Russian composer who reached the United States via Paris, and then after a number of years in this country is once more in France. His early works showed considerable originality and a very special verve which has insured for some of his pieces an enduring popularity. His style is essentially conservative, spiced by cleverly used dissonances.

Toch, Ernst, b. 1887, Vienna — d. 1964, Los Angeles, Calif. Lived for many years in the U. S. Variously characterized as chromaticist, neo-classicist, linear contrapuntist in the Hindemith style. Much well-written, effective piano music.

Turina, Joaquin, b. 1882, Sevilla, Spain—d. 1947, Madrid. Pupil of Vincent d'Indy. Adopted, on Albeniz's advice, a nationalistic orientation in composition. Much striking piano music in Spanish folk idiom.

Villa-Lobos, Heitor, b. 1887, Rio de Janeiro—d. there 1959. Profusely creative, highly original composer, the first South American to achieve world fame. Largely self-taught, he also became a noted pianist and teacher. Most of his works are steeped in Brazilian folklore. Wrote much excellent piano music, including delightful works about childhood.

Webern, Anton, b. 1883, Vienna—d. 1945, Mittersill, Austria (shot by mistake by American occupation troops). A close adherent of Schönberg during the early stages of twelve-tone serial composition. His style is spare, economical, contrapuntal. Only member of the modern "Viennese School" to remain in Vienna.

GLOSSARY

Alcotts, The Third movement of Ives' Second Piano Sonata, subtitled "Concord, Mass. 1840-60". The following description of this movement is a brief excerpt from the composer's preface to this work: "Concord village . . . As one walks down the broad-arched street, passing the white house of Emerson . . . he comes presently beneath the old elms overspreading the Alcott house . . . Within the house . . . there sits the little old spinet-piano Sophie Thoreau gave the Alcott children, on which Beth played the old Scotch airs, and played at the Fifth Symphony . . ."

Arabesque A term borrowed from the decorative designs of Moorish architecture, meaning a composition of rather fanciful melodic contours.

Atonality A twentieth century style of composition in which a definite tonality or key center is lacking; each and every one of the twelve tones of the chromatic scale has equal role and importance.

Bagatelle A short, light piece, usually written for the piano. In this sense, the term was first used by Beethoven.

Bucolics A literary term meaning pastoral poems. In music, pieces of rural, pastoral flavor.

Carillon A percussion instrument consisting of a set of chromatically tuned bells. Also, a piece of music suggesting the sound of this instrument.

Elegy A composition of plaintive or mournful character.

Goyescas A series of seven piano pieces by Granados, inspired by the paintings of Goya. *The Maiden and the Nightingale* is one of them.

Gnossiennes See *Gymnopedies.*

Gymnopedies Satie's Three Gymnopedies and Three Gnossiennes are instrumental pieces in a neo-classical vein, suggesting the modal character and stately ceremonial flavor of the music and dance of ancient Greece.

Impressionism The term is borrowed from a late nineteenth century trend in painting (Manet, Monet, Renoir, and others) according to which the artist presents, or rather suggests, a fleeting impression he gets from a subject at a given moment. Such picture is not objective, not clearly outlined, but rather a highly subjective, hazy, evocative image. A parallel style in music was established largely through the works of Debussy. In his idiom the rules of orthodox harmony, the reign of major and minor tonalities is broken and musical forms are built on a succession of tone colors rather than on the architectural logic of thematic construction.

Invenzione (Invention) A polyphonic piece of two or three voices, usually constructed in imitative counterpoint.

Legende (Legend) A composition of reflective or narrative nature.

Mouvement Plastique Rebikoff's title for a dance piece of graceful plasticity and flexibility.

Passacaglia and Chaconne Closely related baroque instrumental forms in slow triple meter. In essence, they are both a series of variations either on a short, four to eight measure *basso ostinato* melody or on a harmonic sequence of similar length. During the early Baroque the terms are interchangeable; according to later, 18th and 19th century definitions, however, variations on a bass melody are called a Passacaglia, and on a set succession of harmonies, a Chaconne.

Poem A lyric, and often rhapsodic composition.

Polichinelo (Polichinelle, Pulcinella) A buffoon, a puppet clown; also a lively piece of music suggestive of his pranks.

Prelude (Preludium) Literally, a piece of music which serves as an introduction to another piece (such as a fugue) or to a group of pieces (as in the Baroque suite). It is often written in a free form and is of an improvisatory character. Since Chopin, the title is used for a short, independent composition, usually of a lyric, and sometimes of a descriptive nature (Debussy).

Sarabande A stately and solemn old Spanish dance in triple meter. As a part of the baroque suite it usually serves the function of a slow movement.

Serial Technique see Twelve-tone technique.

Siciliana (Sicilienne) An instrumental piece of pastoral character in moderate 6/8 time.

Sonatina A short sonata of simple design. It may consist of one, two or three movements.

Tone Row see Twelve-tone technique.

Twelve-Tone Technique A method of twentieth century composition, a systematization of atonality, devised by Schönberg. A *tone row* or *series,* consisting of all twelve tones of the chromatic scale—arranged in a certain order and manipulated in numerous fashions (retrograde order, inversion, transposition, etc.)—is the basis of twelve-tone technique.

Visions Fugitives (Fleeting Visions) Prokofieff's title for a series of twenty colorful piano pieces in a variety of moods, suggested by a poem of the Russian poet Balmont:
... "In every fleeting vision I see worlds
    Full of the changing play of rainbow hues."

Valsette A little Waltz.

Waltz (Valse, Walzer) The most popular dance of the 19th century and, in different stylized versions, a much cultivated instrumental form of romantic composers. It is a close but more sophisticated relative of the *Ländler* and the *German Dance.* Always in triple time, its tempo, mood and character can vary greatly.